Print Handwriting Workbook for Teens

Practice Workbook with Fun Science Facts that Build Knowledge in a Young Teenager

Legal & Disclaimer

The information contained in this book and its contents are not designed to replace or take the place of any form of medical or professional advice. The information provided by this book is not meant to replace the need for independent medical, financial, legal or other professional advice or services, as may be required.

The content and information contained in this book have been compiled from sources deemed reliable and are accurate to the best of the Author's knowledge and belief. The Author cannot, however, guarantee its accuracy and validity and cannot be held liable for any errors and/or omissions. When needed, further changes will be periodically made to this book. Where appropriate and/or necessary, you agree and are obligated to consult a professional before using any information in this book.

Upon using the contents and information contained in this book, you agree to hold the Author harmless from and against any damages, costs, and expenses, including any legal fees potentially resulting from the application of any of the information provided by this book. This disclaimer applies to any loss, damages or injury caused by the use and application, whether directly or indirectly, of any advice or information presented, whether for breach of contract, tort, negligence, personal injury, criminal intent, or under any other cause of action.

You agree to accept all risks of using the information presented in this book.

Disclaimer Note:
While we try to provide the most accurate information possible.
Please note that each scientific field is subjected to constant discoveries.
That's why the facts included in this book
might be proven wrong or might be updated in the years to come.
However, our goal here is to spark your curiosity and
offer an interesting and enjoyable handwriting experience.

Introduction to Print Handwriting

The goal of this workbook is to help you develop or improve your print handwriting skills. It is designed for beginners and intermediates since it mostly focuses on the writing in print style of entire words and sentences.

This book does, however, contain a short practice section for each letter. This overview includes recommendations on how each letter should be written. The rest of the workbook contains fun and interesting science facts from various fields like:

- *zoology*
- *paleontology*
- *geography*
- *astrology*
- *biology*
- *and many more…*

Each exercise is composed of two sections. The first section contains specific words extracted from the sentence and written with a traceable print font. The second section contains a worksheet designed for the sentence to be rewritten in its entirety (multiple times if possible).

While I highly endorse cursive handwriting because of its scientifically proven benefits. Print handwriting doesn't go without its merits. It can help you develop a neat and legible writing style. It is therefore important, in our modern world, to master both cursive and print handwriting styles. This workbook focuses on the latter.

Each science fact is short and easy to remember. By pairing the benefits of print handwriting with the knowledge from the scientific facts, the value you get from completing each exercise increases radically. In addition, the acquired knowledge can help you start interesting conversations, in your day to day life, with both friends and family.

Print uppercase letters

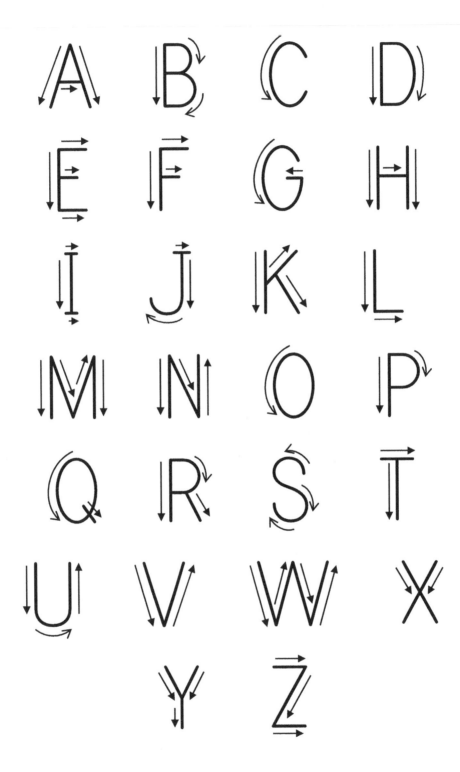

Print lowercase letters

a b c d e f

g h i j k l

m n o p q

r s t u v

w x y z

5

Print letter practice

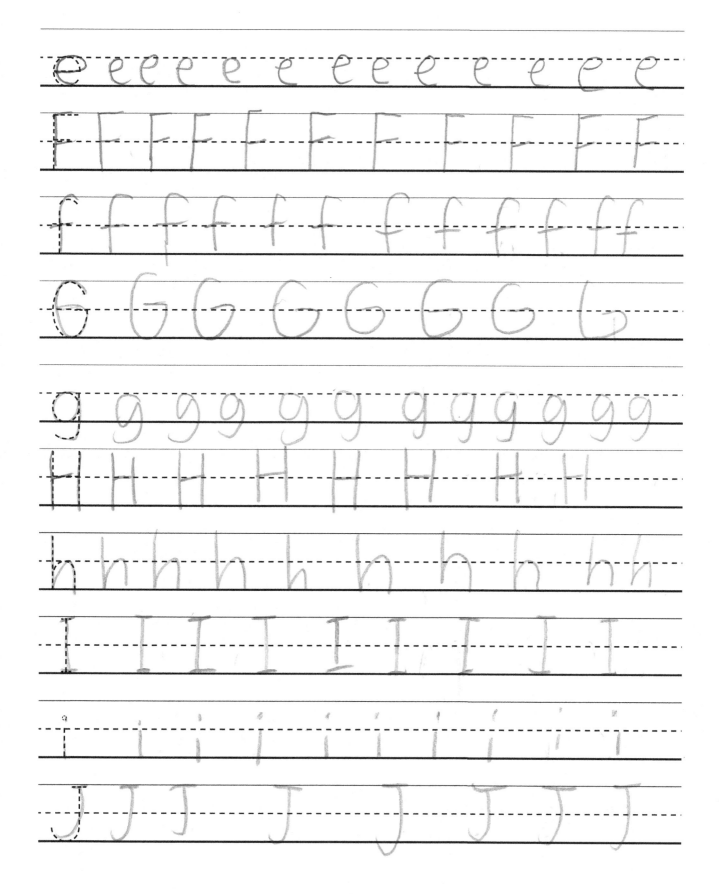

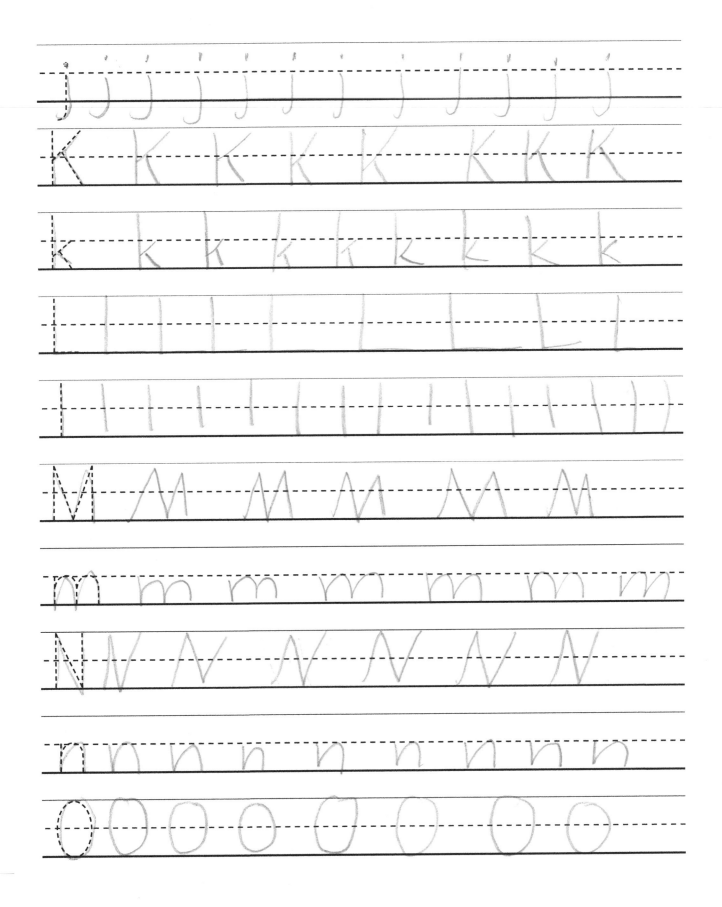

O O O O O O O O O O O O O

P P P P P P P P P

p p p p p p p p p p p p

Q Q Q Q Q Q Q Q Q

q q q q q q q q q q q q q

R

r

S

s

T

Science Fact No.1

The speed of light is 299,792,458 meters per second. That equates to 186,287.49 miles per second.

Copy the entire previous quote below while using your best handwriting.

Science Fact No.2

Light travels from the Sun's surface to the Earth in approximately 8 minutes and 17 seconds.

Light

surface

Earth

minutes

Copy the entire previous quote below while using your best handwriting.

Science Fact No.3

The Earth travels through space at 67,000 miles per hour and simultaneously spins at 1000 miles per hour.

travels

through

space

hour

Copy the entire previous quote below while using your best handwriting.

Science Fact No.4

Over one million earthquakes happen on
Earth every year.

Over

one

million

year

Copy the entire previous quote below while using your best handwriting.

Science Fact No.5

In 1883, the eruption of the volcano Krakatoa was so loud it could be heard 4800 kilometers away in Australia.

eruption

volcano

Krakatoa

heard

Copy the entire previous quote below while using your best handwriting.

Science Fact No.6

The largest recorded hailstone weighed over 1kg and fell in Bangladesh in 1986.

largest

recorded

hailstone

Bangladesh

Copy the entire previous quote below while using your best handwriting.

Science Fact No.7

Around 100 lightning bolts strike the Earth every second.

Around

lightning

bolts

strike

Copy the entire previous quote below while using your best handwriting.

Science Fact No.8

If it were possible to drive your car straight upwards, you would arrive in space in about an hour.

possible

drive

straight

hour

Copy the entire previous quote below while using your best handwriting.

Science Fact No.9

Before the Rockies or the Alps were even formed, the dinosaurs were extinct.

Copy the entire previous quote below while using your best handwriting.

Science Fact No.10

After mating, female black widow spiders eat their male partners.

female

black

widow

spiders

Copy the entire previous quote below while using your best handwriting.

The rate of acceleration of a jumping flea is approximately 20 times that of a space shuttle during launch.

rate

jumping

flea

times

Copy the entire previous quote below while using your best handwriting.

Science Fact No.12

The Kakadu Plum, found in Australia, contains 100 times more vitamin C than an orange.

Kakadu

Plum

vitamin

orange

Copy the entire previous quote below while using your best handwriting.

Science Fact No.13

The Swiss biologist and physician, Friedrich Miescher, discovered DNA in the year of 1869.

Swiss

biologist

physician

discovered

Copy the entire previous quote below while using your best handwriting.

James Watson and Francis Crick
were the first to determine the
molecular structure of DNA in 1953.

first

determine

molecular

structure

Copy the entire previous quote below while using your best handwriting.

Galileo invented the thermometer in 1607.

Copy the entire previous quote below while using your best handwriting.

The magnifying glass was invented by Englishman Roger Bacon in the year 1250.

magnifying

glass

invented

year

Copy the entire previous quote below while using your best handwriting.

Science Fact No.17

Dynamite was invented by Alfred Nobel in 1866.

Copy the entire previous quote below while using your best handwriting.

Wilhelm Rontgen discovered X-rays in 1895. For that achievement, he was awarded the Nobel Prize for physics.

awarded

Nobel

Prize

physics

Copy the entire previous quote below while using your best handwriting.

The tallest tree ever (an Australian eucalyptus) was measured at 435 feet (132.6 meters) in 1872.

tallest

tree

Australian

eucalyptus

Copy the entire previous quote below while using your best handwriting.

Science Fact No.20

The sun will turn into a Red Giant in around 5 billion years when it will run out of fuel.

sun

Red

Giant

fuel

Copy the entire previous quote below while using your best handwriting.

Science Fact No.21

Giraffes often sleep for only 20 minutes during a 24-hour period.

Giraffes

often

sleep

minutes

Copy the entire previous quote below while using your best handwriting.

Science Fact No.22

The earliest winemakers lived around 7000 BC in China.

Copy the entire previous quote below while using your best handwriting.

Science Fact No.23

It takes about 60 seconds for an individual blood cell to make a complete circuit of the body.

takes

seconds

individual

cell

Copy the entire previous quote below while using your best handwriting.

Science Fact No.24

Alexander Graham Bell is credited with inventing and patenting the first practical telephone. On the day he was buried, the entire US telephone system was shut down for 1 minute in tribute to him.

credited

inventing

practical

telephone

Copy the entire previous quote below while using your best handwriting.

The loudest noise made by a living creature is the low frequency call of the humpback whale.

Copy the entire previous quote below while using your best handwriting.

Science Fact No.26

The eyes of giant squids are the largest of any living creature on Earth (up to 10 inches in diameter).

eyes

giant

squids

creature

Copy the entire previous quote below while using your best handwriting.

Science Fact No.27

The Universe contains over 2 trillion galaxies.

Universe

contains

trillion

galaxies

Copy the entire previous quote below while using your best handwriting.

The largest galaxy discovered (to the date this fact was written) has about 100 trillion stars.

Copy the entire previous quote below while using your best handwriting.

Science Fact No.29

The fastest speed at which a falling raindrop can hit you is 18 miles per hour (28.9 kilometers per hour).

Copy the entire previous quote below while using your best handwriting.

The Tanzanian parasitic wasp is the world's smallest winged insect and is smaller than the eye of a housefly.

Tanzanian

wasp

smallest

winged

Copy the entire previous quote below while using your best handwriting.

Every year, the grey whale migrates 12,500 miles from the Arctic to Mexico and back.

whale

migrates

Arctic

Mexico

Copy the entire previous quote below while using your best handwriting.

Science Fact No.32

A sloth typically sleeps for 15 to 20 hours a day.

sloth

typically

sleeps

hours

Copy the entire previous quote below while using your best handwriting.

Science Fact No.33

The koala is the sleepiest animal on Earth. It sleeps for an average of 22 hours a day.

koala

sleepiest

average

day

Copy the entire previous quote below while using your best handwriting.

Science Fact No.34

Light would require 0.13 seconds to travel around the Earth.

Light

would

require

seconds

Copy the entire previous quote below while using your best handwriting.

The Universe expands by a billion miles in all directions every single hour.

expands

billion

miles

directions

Copy the entire previous quote below while using your best handwriting.

Science Fact No.36

The driest inhabited place in the world is Aswan, located in Egypt. The annual average rainfall is .02 inches.

Copy the entire previous quote below while using your best handwriting.

Science Fact No.37

The largest dinosaur ever discovered was called the Seismosaurus. It was over 100 feet long and weighed up to 80 tonnes.

largest

dinosaur

feet

weighed

Copy the entire previous quote below while using your best handwriting.

Science Fact No.38

In order to escape the Earth's gravity, a rocket needs to travel at a speed of at least 7 miles per second.

escape

gravity

rocket

travel

Copy the entire previous quote below while using your best handwriting.

The world's largest butterfly is the Queen Alexandra's Birdwing. It has a wingspan of up to 12 inches.

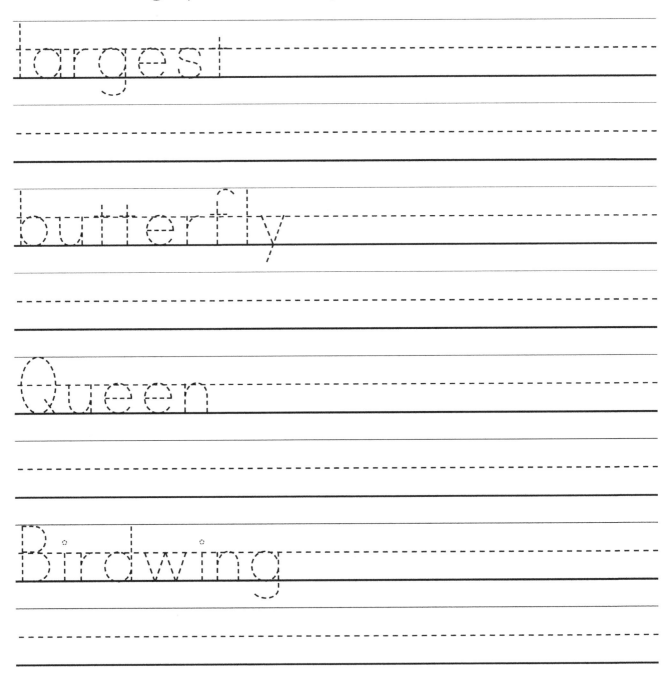

Copy the entire previous quote below while using your best handwriting.

Science Fact No.40

The human body contains enough carbon to create 9000 pencils.

human

body

contains

carbon

Copy the entire previous quote below while using your best handwriting.

Science Fact No.41

Humans cannot taste food without the presence of saliva.

Humans

cannot

taste

without

Copy the entire previous quote below while using your best handwriting.

Galapagos tortoises, the largest of all
living tortoises, can live to be well
over 100 years old.

Galapagos

tortoises

largest

living

Copy the entire previous quote below while using your best handwriting.

Ants are capable of carrying objects
that are 50 times heavier than their
own body weight.

Ants

capable

carrying

objects

Copy the entire previous quote below while using your best handwriting.

Science Fact No.44

Penguins have better eyesight underwater than on land.

Penguins

better

eyesight

underwater

Copy the entire previous quote below while using your best handwriting.

Science Fact No.45

A lightning strike can reach a temperature of approximately 30,000 °C (54,000 °F).

lightning

strike

can

reach

Copy the entire previous quote below while using your best handwriting.

Made in the USA
Coppell, TX
23 August 2020

34509935R00057